Rivers in the Rain Forest

Saviour Pirotta

WAYLAND

Deep in the Rain Forest

PEOPLE in the Rain Forest

PREDATORS in the Rain Forest

RIVERS in the Rain Forest

TREES AND PLANTS in the Rain Forest

Cover picture: Children paddle their canoe in a flooded village in Brazil.

Title page: Boys having fun jumping in the Amazon river, during the annual flood in Amazonas State, Brazil.

Contents page: The Rio Negro in Brazil during the rainy season.

Editor: Polly Goodman
Designer: Tim Mayer
Consultant: Michael S. Dilger Bsc (Hons) Msc

First published in 1998 by
Wayland Publishers Ltd
61 Western Road, Hove
East Sussex BN3 1JD, England

Find Wayland on the Internet at
http://www.wayland.co.uk

British Library Cataloguing in Publication Data
Pirotta, Saviour, 1958–
    Rivers in the rain forest.
    – (Deep in the rain forest)
    1. Rivers – Juvenile literature
    2. Rainforest ecology – Juvenile literature
    I. Title
    577.6'4

ISBN 0 7502 2199 2

Printed and bound in Italy by LEGO S.p.A., Vicenza

Contents

Rain Forests around the World

Rain forests are thick forests in parts of the world where there is lots of rain. Most rain forests are near the Equator, an imaginary line that runs around the centre of the earth. The largest rain forest is the Amazon, in South America.

◀ Mudskippers live in East and West Africa, India, Indonesia and northern Australia.

◀ Gold can be found in rainforest rivers in Indonesia and the Amazon.

EQUATOR

◀ Carving canoes are essential skills to people who live near rainforest rivers.

Rivers flow through every rain forest. The Amazon is the biggest river in the world. It flows through the Amazon rain forest. The Orinoco river cuts across rain forest in Colombia and Venezuela. The Congo river flows through rain forest in Central Africa.

◀ Tourists on a rainforest river trip up the Carrao river, in Venezuela.

KEY

 The green areas on the map show rain forests.

▲ Catfish are important food for people in the rain forest.

▲ Cows on rafts in a flooded village in the Amazon of Brazil.

Rivers of Life

Rivers are essential to rain forests. They provide the forests with water all year round. Rivers also provide a home to many different plants and animals. People rely on the rivers, too.

▼ Clouds hang over the Manu river in the Amazon, Peru.

▲ People in rain forests are used to lots of heavy rain. This boy is using a palm leaf as an umbrella.

The water cycle

Water from rivers is always on the move. The hot sun heats the rivers, and turns the water into a gas, called water vapour. The water vapour rises up to the sky.

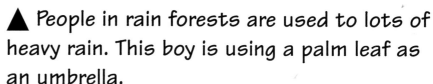

7

In the sky, the water vapour cools down. It turns back into water and forms clouds. When the water in the clouds becomes too heavy, it falls as rain.

Some of the rainwater is used by the trees and plants for growth. Other water seeps back into the rivers. The journey of water between the rivers, trees and clouds is called the water cycle.

▼ Rising mists and clouds over rain forest in Malaysia.

The water cycle

2. The water vapour cools and forms clouds.

3. The water vapour turns back into liquid and falls as rain.

1. The sun heats the water in rivers and plants. It turns into vapour and rises up in the air.

4. Rainwater seeps through the trees, flows back into the rivers or goes underground.

River Plants

Mangrove trees grow in swamps, at the mouths of rainforest rivers. Mangroves have special long roots, which help anchor them in the mud.

Mangrove seeds sprout on the branches of their mother tree, instead of in the ground. This means they are not washed away by the tide before they can grow into saplings.

▲ Mangrove seeds sprouting on their mother tree.

▼ The roots of mangrove trees in Belize.

Giant water lilies grow in rainforest rivers. Some grow big enough for a small child to sit on.

Victoria water lilies grow in shallow water. Some can grow up to 2 metres wide.

▲ Victoria water lilies in the Amazon.

Animals in Rivers

The rivers of the rain forest are home to many different fish, amphibians, reptiles and mammals.

The mudskipper lives in the mangroves. It is a fish, but it can also breathe out of water. Mudskippers use their fins to walk as well as swim.

▼ Two male mudskippers look at each other angrily, with their fins raised.

Basilisks are amphibians. They are also called Jesus lizards because they can walk on water!

Basilisks have long webbed toes on their back feet which act as paddles. They can run across small streams on their back legs.

▲ A basilisk, or Jesus lizard, running across a stream.

13

Animals as food

There are over 2,400 types of fish in the Amazon. Catfish are one of the largest. They can grow over 2 metres long. Catfish are very important food for people.

The manatee is the biggest animal in the Amazon river. Manatees move very slowly, feeding on grasses on the riverbed.

▲ A fisherman with a huge catfish he has just caught, in the Manu river, Peru.

▼ Manatees hold their breath for up to 15 minutes when they swim underwater.

Flood!

Rivers in rain forests often burst their banks, and deep water covers the forest floor. This means that fish can get to parts of the forest they cannot usually reach.

Arowana fish are known by local fishermen as 'water monkies', because they jump out of the water. They leap up to 2 metres above the water to catch beetles, spiders, and even birds and bats.

Arowana fish have ▶ large mouths, so they can swallow animals as big as birds.

The tambaqui fish particularly likes the seeds of the January palm tree. It can only reach them when the forest floor is flooded. The tambaqui cracks the seeds with its big flat teeth.

▲ Two tambaqui fish swimming up to a January palm to eat its seeds.

People and floods

Most people in rain forests are used to the floods. Some people build their houses on stilts. Others build houses like boats, which float on the water when the rivers flood.

▼ Houses on stilts in the Amazon, surrounded by flooded forest.

▲ Cattle graze on rafts, during the yearly flood of the Amazon, in Brazil.

When the water-level rises, some farmers put their animals on rafts tied to the river bank. The animals have to be careful not to fall in the water, where hungry piranhas could get them!

River Roads

Many rainforest people use the rivers to get around. It is easier to travel on the rivers than fighting through thick forest.

▼ This man is using an axe to hollow out a canoe, in Papua New Guinea.

The smallest boats on the rivers are canoes. They are made by hollowing out tree trunks. Richer people sometimes have motors attached to them.

▲ Canoes are the only way to get around in this flooded village.

Canoes are used to get to school, to riverside markets and by fishermen.

Carrying goods

On giant rainforest rivers, big freighters carry rubber, beef and mineral ore to busy ports. Smaller boats are used to carry animals, coffee beans and bananas to riverside markets. Big logs are tied together to make huge rafts and towed downstream.

▼ Huge logs are towed down a river on a raft in the Amazon, Brazil.

▼ Canoes carry goods to a riverside market in Colombia.

Mining

People have made their fortune by finding gold or diamonds in rainforest rivers.

Prospectors sift through the earth from riverbeds, looking for precious stones. They use special pans or dishes, which separate the stones from the sand.

◀ A prospector looking for gold in Indonesia.

24

Mining causes a lot of damage to rivers. It disturbs the water at riverbanks, where fish and other animals come to drink.

Prospectors drop mercury into the water, to help separate the stones. Since mercury is poisonous, it kills fish and animals in the rivers. Mercury can poison people, too.

▼ These gold miners are disturbing the banks of the Sekonyer river in Indonesia by looking for gold.

Saving the rivers

Rivers are being polluted by mining. We need to save the rivers, so that people can enjoy them in the future.

Tourists can take trips down the rivers and find out all about rain forests, without causing harm. They also bring money into poor areas.

You can help by finding out as much as you can about rain forests. There might be something you can do.

▼ This part of the Amazon rain forest has been destroyed by gold miners.

▼ Tourists on a river trip in Venezuela.

Make a Rainforest Canoe

Brown card, or card painted brown

Tracing paper

A pencil

Scissors

Sticky tape

Make your own miniature rainforest canoe by following these simple steps:

1. Trace the patterns on the right on to tracing paper and cut them out.

Then place the patterns on to brown card and cut the patterns out of the card.

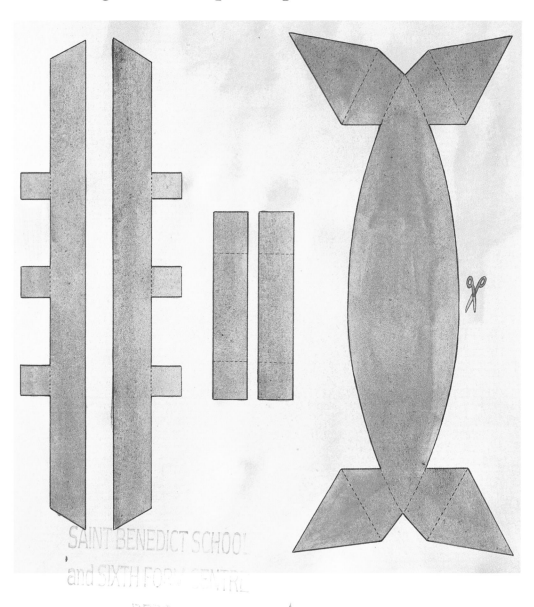

SAINT BENEDICT SCHOOL
and SIXTH FORM CENTRE
DERBY

2. Fold up the ends of the canoe base, one after the other. Stick the edges together with sticky tape.

3. Add the sides of the canoe, putting them inside each end, and fasten them with sticky tape on the bottom.

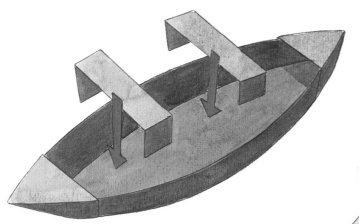

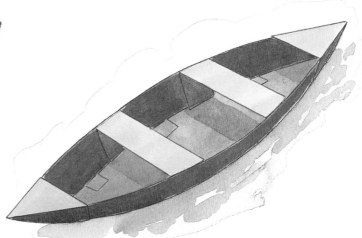

4. Now you can add the seats. Fold the edges of the seats and stick them on to the inside of the canoe.

5. Now see if your canoe will float! You could have a race with a friend by blowing your canoes across a bath of water.

Further Information

Other books to read

Animals by Habitat: Animals of the Rain Forest by Stephen Savage (Wayland, 1996)

Look Who Lives in the Rain Forest by Alan Baker (MacDonald Young Books, 1998)

People and Places in Peril: Rainforests by Sara Oldfield (Cherrytree Books, 1995)

Rainforests Animals by D. Alderton (Ladybird, 1995)

World of the Rain Forest by Rosie McCormick (TwoCan, 1997)

Worldwise: Rainforest by Penny Clarke (Watts, 1996)

CD Rom

Exploring Land Habitats (Wayland, 1997)

Audio tape

Environmental Sounds: Tropical Jungle (The Nature Company Tel: 001 510 644 1337) – recordings from the Amazon, including a rainstorm passing overhead, a jaguar's roar and spider monkey's chatter.

Useful addresses

All these groups provide material on rain forests for schools:

Friends of the Earth (UK)
26-28 Underwood Street, London N1 7QJ
Tel: 0171 490 1555
Internet: www. for.co.uk/

Living Earth Foundation
4 Great James Street
London WC1N 3DA
Tel: 0171 242 3816
Internet: http://www.gn.apc.org/Living Earth

Reforest The Earth
42–46 Bethel Street,
Norwich NR2 1NR
Tel: 01603 611953

Worldwide Fund for Nature
Panda House
Wayside Park
Cattleshall Lane
Godalming GU7 1XR
Tel: 01608 676691
Internet: http://www.wwf-uk.org

Picture acknowledgements
Bruce Coleman Ltd (Luiz Claudio Marigo) *cover, title page* , 21, (Jane Burton) 4 (top left), 12 , (Alain Compost) 4 (top right), 24, (Andrew Davies) 10 -11 (middle), Luiz Claudio Marigo) 19; Ecoscene (W. Lawler) 25; Robert Harding (K. Gillham) 22; NHPA (Martin Wendler) *contents page*, (Stephen Dalton) 13, (Jany Sauvanet) 26; Oxford Scientific Films (Michael Pitts) 4 (bottom), 20, (Harold Taylor Abipp) 8, (Max Gibbs) 16, (Nick Gordon) 17 (right); Panos Pictures (Jeremy Horner) 23; Planet Earth Pictures (Andrew Bartachi) 14; South American Pictures (Tony Morrison) 10 (left), 18; Still Pictures (Adi-Unep) 7 (top); Tony Stone Images (Kevin Schafer) 5 (top), 27, (Frans Lanting) 5 (bottom left), (Stuart Westmorland) 5 (bottom right), 15, (Frans Lanting) 6-7 (bottom); Wayland Picture library 11 (right). Border and folio artwork: Kate Davenport. World map and water-cycle artwork: Peter Bull.

Topic Web and Notes

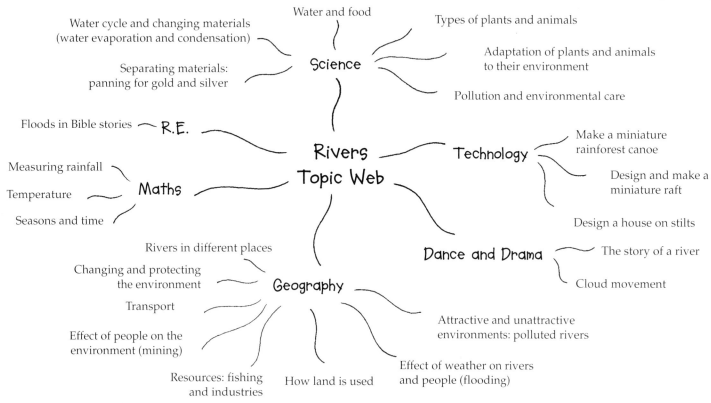

Water cycle and changing materials
(water evaporation and condensation)

Water and food

Types of plants and animals

Separating materials:
panning for gold and silver

Science

Adaptation of plants and animals
to their environment

Pollution and environmental care

Floods in Bible stories — R.E.

Rivers
Topic Web

Technology

Make a miniature
rainforest canoe

Measuring rainfall

Design and make a
miniature raft

Temperature

Maths

Seasons and time

Design a house on stilts

Dance and Drama

The story of a river

Rivers in different places

Cloud movement

Changing and protecting
the environment

Geography

Transport

Effect of people on the
environment (mining)

Attractive and unattractive
environments: polluted rivers

Resources: fishing
and industries

How land is used

Effect of weather on rivers
and people (flooding)

GEOGRAPHY

● Compare your local river to one in the rainforest. Which one is the biggest and the longest? What vegetation surrounds it? What types of transport use it? Make a chart showing the similarities and differences between the two.

● How many different work activities can you find in this book? Make a list of products that are obtained from rainforest rivers.

SCIENCE

● Find pictures of different types of boats in the rainforest. Which are the fastest and which are the slowest? Why? What are they used for?

● Look at the different animals in this book. Divide them into fish, mammals and amphibians.

● Discuss what would happen if the local river flooded. How would it differ from flooding in the rain forest?

● Discuss how people are destroying the rain forest. Collect news articles from books, magazines, newspapers and the Internet. Find out ways of protecting the rain forests.

DRAMA AND DANCE

● Make up a mime or a play tracing the journey of a river from its source to the sea.

● Make up a dance showing the movement of water in the water cycle. Use page 9 to help.

DESIGN AND TECHNOLOGY

● Using only paper and a pencil, twigs and string, design and make a miniature raft. You can use the picture on page 22 to help. Test the raft in a sink to make sure it floats.

R.E.

● Stories of floods are found in the writings of every major religion. Using the information in this book, make up your own 'flood' story, with a message of sharing.

ENGLISH

● Write a diary describing a day's fishing in the Amazon, using the information found in this book.

31

Glossary

Amphibians Animals that live on land and in water.

Cycle A pattern of events which repeat themselves.

Freighter A big ship that carries goods, such as food or minerals.

Mangroves Tropical trees, which grow in mud and can survive when they are covered by sea-water.

Mercury A poisonous liquid metal.

Mineral ore Rock with valuable metals inside.

Mouth The part of the river where it meets the sea.

Prospectors People who look for minerals and precious stones in the ground, to sell for money.

Saplings Young trees.

Swamps Wet, marshy ground.

Tides The rise and fall of the surface of the sea.

Water vapour Water that is heated up and turned into a gas.

Webbed Joined together.

Index

Page numbers in **bold** show there is a picture on the page as well as information.